The What and How of

PTSD:

Understanding and *Moving Beyond*

Céline Paris
M.Ps., C. Psych., Psychologist

 FriesenPress

Suite 300 - 990 Fort St
Victoria, BC, V8V 3K2
Canada

www.friesenpress.com

Copyright © 2016 by Céline Paris
First Edition — 2016

"The wave is the perfect image for your book, a signature image. There is no-one more courageous than a sailor. Talk to a captain of a ship or a fisherman and they will tell you that there is nothing more terrifying than a storm at sea. But they face it. They see that wave and they don't back down because they know that if they do, they pay with their life so they steer into it and follow the tempo until the storm passes. They never give up. That is exactly what someone battling PTSD, a survivor, must do." – Canadian Forces Veteran who overcame PTSD

ISBN
978-1-4602-8232-8 (Hardcover)
978-1-4602-8233-5 (Paperback)
978-1-4602-8234-2 (eBook)

1. PSYCHOLOGY, PSYCHOPATHOLOGY, POST-TRAUMATIC STRESS DISORDER (PTSD)

Distributed to the trade by The Ingram Book Company

"Evolution has designed for us a really difficult brain, one that can create heaven or hell, and it's up to each of us to choose which to opt for. Opening our hearts to each other and developing self-kindness based on understanding that 'none of us chooses to be here with this strange mind' is probably not a bad first step."

Paul Gilbert

"You are not responsible for being down, but you are responsible for **getting up.**"

—Jesse Jackson

Acknowledgments

Thank you to my brave patients. You know who you are. I hope you know what it has meant to me, that you have opened your hearts and shared your stories with me.

Mille mercis à Pascale B. de son aide précieuse, son bel exemple, et aussi d'avoir cru en ce projet dès le tout début.

"The world breaks everyone, but some are **stronger** in the broken places."

—Ernest Hemingway

Table of Contents

Foreword

A picture is worth a thousand words.

Chinese proverb

Dear Reader,

I am a psychologist. I have been working with patients diagnosed with post-traumatic stress disorder (mostly soldiers) for more decades than I care to say. This picture book was built around three diagrams developed to help teach these patients and their loved ones about their symptoms. My goal is to explain PTSD in order to aid recovery and weaken stigma—I am convinced that once a person suffering from PTSD understands what is really happening inside his or her mind, shame loses its grip.

If you have been diagnosed with PTSD, this book was written for you. If someone you love struggles with this disorder, this book was also written with you in mind.

You are reading on—terrific.

If you have PTSD, your concentration will probably be an issue. I did my very best to make the information as easy to grasp as possible. But if you find yourself put off by psychological terms such as "appraisal," please bear with me. I don't want to water down the information and I tried to make up for the dryness by breaking the text up with pictures. I chose each picture to illustrate a point or a metaphor. I turned them into watercolours to soften them—that way their style and content carry little risk of triggering your symptoms.

Please feel free to use this book in any way you wish. You can go straight to the headings or pictures that grab your interest and then tackle the rest in small bites. There is no right or wrong way to take in new information.

By all means, share this book with those closest to you. I sincerely hope it will help spark some good conversations and deepen understanding.

Typically, you don't understand what is happening when you first experience the symptoms of PTSD. The same thing goes for witnessing them happening to someone you care about. That's natural. My goal is simple: to answer your initial questions and pave the way for therapy.

If you love someone with PTSD, this book is for you too. Readers may have noticed already that I have decided to address the person with PTSD directly, using the pronoun "you." I hope this does not make others feel as though I am forgetting them. My intention is to draw in the person with the symptoms in every way possible. If you are reading because a loved one suffers from PTSD, please know that my use of "you" is meant to be inclusive.

All of the therapies that work start with good psycho-education: the purpose of this book is to take care of that first step in a user-friendly way. There are many other books to cover the next steps. I have a few recommendations in the Resource section at the end of this book.

If you discover part way through that reading this kind of book is not really for you, there are many other ways to make sense of what you are dealing with. Just don't give up. Please get the help you need. In case you need to bail, the four most important things I want you to know are:

It is not your fault
You are not alone
PTSD happens in the brain
Therapy works

"If only we could wear bandages on the outside for the wounds we have on the inside!"

Message from Rick, a soldier. He drew this at the time that he was struggling with PTSD to make the point that it is an invisible injury that needs to be seen and understood.

Each section will expand on these key messages. The longest and most information-packed section, the core of the book, is Part Three: PTSD Happens in the Brain.

Dear reader, whoever you are—friend, family, helper, sufferer, survivor—if you make it to the end of this book, wonderful. You will have gained the essential information to understand PTSD.

Part One

It's Not Your Fault

The first things you need to know about PTSD

What did you feel before you understood what was happening to you? If you knew about post-trauma effects already, did you think PTSD was for a certain type of person, somebody weak or "emotional," for example, or someone in a certain line of work? Even now, do you understand, truly understand, why and how it happened to you?

You probably know by now that PTSD refers to distress that follows a major stressful life event. The definition of trauma from the *Diagnostic and Statistical Manual of Mental Disorders (DSM-5®)*[1] is "exposure to actual or threatened death, serious injury or sexual violence," which covers a wide range of difficult human experiences. It is important to understand that it can happen to anyone, given certain circumstances. Here are three examples. See if one or more sound like you.

---

[1] American Psychiatric Association, 2013. *Diagnostic and Statistical Manual of Mental Disorders (DSM-5˚)*, Arlington, VA: APA Publishing.

Three stories of PTSD

Anne

"Why am I not getting over this? I'm fine."

Anne, a bank manager, has not been the same since a burglary in her home. She was held at knifepoint and left tied to a chair for hours before a neighbour found her. Fortunately, she was unharmed.

Anne thinks she has been lucky, but then the nightmares and fears return. Initially, her family and friends rallied around her, but as the weeks turned into months they seem to expect her to "just get over it." Their lack of understanding makes her retreat into herself more and more.

Martin

"I'm a helper. This can't be happening to me."

Martin is a peacekeeper. He is a medical assistant, and a good one. He is trained to help people who are suffering; he is also trained as a soldier. He came through the horrors of Rwanda.

Then, on a tour to Bosnia years later, he witnessed the suffering of a boy about the same age as his son. This brings vivid images of the pain and death he saw years before in Rwanda to the forefront. He fights the symptoms as hard as he can and finishes the tour, even though he is not sleeping. He relives Rwanda every day and night in one way or another.

After his return he goes through the motions at home and at work. It is his temper that finally gives him away. His wife urges him to get help, but how can he? His career is at stake. Besides, it is he who is the helper.

Nicholas

"Let this be a heart attack, not PTSD."

Nicholas is a firefighter (though he could be a police officer or an emergency medical responder) nearing the end of a long career. He knows better than anyone the importance of keeping a cool head. He has seen more death and suffering than he cares to remember, but he has also saved many, many lives.

Without warning, during a movie with a fiery crash scene, he has to leave the theatre because of chest pain and shortness of breath. His wife takes him to the emergency room, worried about his heart.

The doctor reassures him that it is "only" a panic attack. Nicholas is ashamed, taking this to mean that it is "all in his head." He knows about PTSD, of course. He's had the training at work and seen colleagues go on sick leave. Could this be the beginning?

"Come to think of it," Nicholas thinks, "I'll take the heart condition."

Do any of these stories sound like you? Can you identify with Anne, Martin, or Nicholas? Despite their differences, all three feel out of control and are asking themselves, "What is going on?"

Because her symptoms started right after a traumatic incident where her life was threatened, Anne and her family have a good idea of the origin of her problem. Reasoning that nothing really happened in the end, in the sense that she wasn't physically harmed, she and her family wonder why she doesn't get better and why her home no longer feels safe.

Martin and Nicholas have chosen dangerous occupations. They have learned through experience that they can cope with a lot. Martin thought he would be okay because his own life was never in danger. He doesn't know about helplessness. Nicholas also thought he was protected because he had coped so well at the time of the crises. He doesn't know about delayed reactions.

PTSD is a great equalizer. It doesn't matter whether you "got" it from war, accident, crime, or something else. Once it is with you, the differences stop being important. The similarities are what stand out, because the symptoms are pretty much the same. They vary in degree, but not in nature. One exception is childhood trauma, especially childhood sexual abuse. Trauma happening at a very young age can affect personality as it is developing and the impact tends to be particularly profound and complex.

I often hear people say that they don't deserve to have PTSD, because they didn't do anything brave like rescue someone or fight for their country, or because their own life was not threatened. This thinking is misdirected—please don't go there. Trauma can happen anywhere, to anyone, and while there are things that can certainly bolster one's resilience, such as experience and training, nobody is immune.

Anne, Martin, and Nicholas need information. They say knowledge is power, and that is what they need to regain control of their lives. And they need to find hope.

What is PTSD, actually?

Responses to stress and to traumatic experiences affect both the body and the mind. In humans, this involves two fundamentally different ways of knowing, two levels of information processing, two systems working together to make up the normal stress response. They get badly out of synch with PTSD. These are explained in more detail later in the book.

People who suffer from PTSD describe it best. They say things like: "I can't seem to control my mind anymore. I start reliving the worst day in my life at the most inopportune times. There is no warning, it is like a switch is being flipped." Or, "I am so ashamed…I try to hide my reactions from everyone, even my wife. Especially my wife. How can I make her understand what I don't understand myself? It's like I've lost my mind." Or, "The worst thing about this is my temper. I swear someday I'm going to take somebody down. I almost hit my child when he snuck up on me to play a game. I'm just going to have to isolate myself for others' protection." Or, "I can't believe this is happening to me. I can't face people any more. I used to be so confident. Now a family gathering is an ordeal. I go to the store for necessities only. I make excuses not to go to the mall."

Researchers who have studied PTSD can shed some light onto what is actually happening. Some have called PTSD a "normal reaction to an abnormal event," but you will see that it is a bit more complicated than that. PTSD is not simply about trauma; it is about not recovering after trauma.

Persons whose lives have been threatened or who have seen others killed, hurt, or endangered, can and do experience very strong emotions—fear, horror and / or helplessness—at the time of the event.

Some recover fully, while others do not. It is when these intense emotions do not fade, and the symptoms of distress last more than one month that PTSD may be suspected.

Why me?

The reasons why one person develops PTSD and another does not remain a bit of a mystery to this day. The severity of the trauma and the number of traumatic events in a person's life are important predictors. Psychologists call this the "dose" effect—the bigger the dose, the higher the risk. But that is not the whole story.

The event is not the direct cause of PTSD, but most people do not know or appreciate this fully. A stressful event leads to PTSD in circumstances where the normal stress response becomes stuck. This happens also with depression; grief and loss do not cause depression, but they can lead to it. Depression is an illness that can be understood as a complication of the normal grieving process.

Some psychologists compare PTSD to a wound that is not healing properly on its own and needs medical attention, such as an antibiotic.

One thing is certain: a person's courage or moral strength is not a predictor of PTSD.

Regardless of how effectively you functioned during the crisis or how bravely you handled the danger, you may still develop PTSD and be bothered by symptoms long after the danger has passed.

In fact, courageous people put themselves in harm's way more than others, so it makes sense that their risk is probably higher. Unfortunately, valour cannot neutralize strong, natural emotions like fear and helplessness.

Why? Because emotions and behaviour are two different things. Behaviour can be controlled, but feelings cannot, at least not directly.

Emotions vs. behaviour

Emotions are a bit like the weather. When pleasant, they can just be enjoyed, but at other times they can be truly disruptive. Unlike the weather, though, they are not intrinsically dangerous. There are ways to limit the impact of both, and anyone can tap into this knowledge. The first step is acceptance—letting go of the desire to control them. That means giving up on trying to fight, stop, or avoid them and letting them simply wash over you instead. Easier said than done, I know.

For this, you have to see feelings for what they are: fleeting events that are not under your control. A guided meditation that I like invites you to imagine that you are the sky and your emotions are the clouds passing by. This helps you to grasp that it is possible to observe your emotions and not get caught up in them. It requires a lot of practice, but it can be done.

Emotions come in waves—did you know this? The worst ones rarely last more than twenty minutes. If you have had a major loss, like the death of someone you loved, you may remember that you didn't cry (or ache in stoic silence if that's your style) all the time. There were probably breaks. The sadness comes in great crashing waves. Over time, the waves lessen. There are fewer at one month, or one year, than on the first day. The best way to handle these waves is not to try to fight them or block them—that is exhausting as well as ineffective—but to imagine floating above them in a boat, or riding them like a surfer. It's a paradox: if you let them be, they leave faster.

What you flee pursues you, but what you face dissipates.

Morrie, the teacher who is dying of ALS in *Tuesdays with Morrie,* tells author Mitch Albom that first you let yourself feel the fear, the sadness, whatever—you "bathe" in it if you have to—then, and only then, can you detach from it and go on to feel the other emotions of life. [2] Martha Beck, whose concise *"Guide to Avoiding Avoidance"* can be found online, says it best: "Emotional discomfort, when accepted, rises, crests and falls in a series of waves. It's different from unwilling suffering the way the sting of disinfectant is different from the sting of decay; the pain leaves you healthier than it found you."

---

2   Mitch Albom, 2002. *Tuesdays with Morrie: An Old Man, a Young Man, and Life's Greatest Lesson.* New York: Broadway Books.

The four clusters of symptoms of PTSD

It can be helpful to you to understand what health professionals look for when they diagnose PTSD, and learn some of our lingo. It is also helpful to put names to the symptoms that you are experiencing. The latest version of the *DSM-5®* groups the main symptoms that trouble the person with PTSD into four "clusters."

I. **Intrusion:** reliving the event in dreams, vivid, unwanted memories, or flashbacks	**2.** **Avoidance:** efforts to stay away from or push away reminders of the trauma
3. **Detachment and numbness:** changes in thoughts or moods associated with the event	**4.** **Hyper-arousal:** the body cannot relax, and the mind cannot focus effectively

Part Two

You are not Alone

Trauma has been part of life for as long as humanity has existed. There have always been wars, infant mortality, predators, famine, natural disasters, epidemics, and accidents. Humans have found ways to move beyond loss and pain and terror. They've had to.

Clearly, many, many others have been down a road like yours. Most have eventually found a way to a better life. It probably didn't seem possible to them when they first started.

You do realize that there is no surefire way to escape pain and suffering? Even if you chose to live in a cabin in the woods and made sure you didn't become attached to any living thing, you might avoid the pain of loss or rejection, but you would suffer from loneliness and boredom. You would be trading one kind of pain for another.

Many people with PTSD feel they are so changed that no one will understand them. This is simply not true. The best example is art. Trauma inspired some the greatest creative works of all time, like Shakespeare's tragedies, Picasso's Guernica, and Michelangelo's La Pieta. Everywhere in the world, artists have brought to life the whole range of human emotions - love and loss, joy and pain. The wide appeal of great works of art proves that sharing even difficult emotions is natural for humans. Art - literature, painting, music – deepens our empathy for one another. It makes us feel connected, understood, and part of something greater than ourselves.

Perhaps you think that it is a kindness to keep your difficult experience and your pain to yourself, that it protects your loved ones. Don't be so sure. They know something is wrong, but they don't know why and their theories are often worse than the truth. Shakespeare, who knew the human condition in all its glory, wrote, "Present fears are less than horrible imaginings." (Macbeth, Act I, Scene III.)

We now know that social connection is the greatest predictor of happiness. And when you face trauma, even if there is a lot that we still don't know about PTSD, one very important thing that we do know is this: social support matters.

If at the same time you encounter trauma you happen to be going through a breakup, or your friends are distant, or someone you care about lays blame on you, you are at greater risk of developing PTSD.

Conversely, social support is protective. Those who survive life challenges the best are those who increase their social contacts, not those who pull away. There is now conclusive scientific evidence that asking for support and allowing yourself to receive it is just about the healthiest thing you can do.

It makes sense when you think about it. As health psychologist Kelly McGonigal points out in her wonderful TEDTalk, *How to Make Stress Your Friend,*[3], we are social animals, so evolution gave our stress response a built-in mechanism for stress resilience—human connection.

Dr. McGonigal says that when we humans reach out to others under stress, whether to seek support or to help someone else, we release more of a certain stress hormone called oxytocin, which is just as important as adrenaline or cortisol. This hormone drives us to "tend and befriend." Its action makes our stress response healthier, helps our bodies heal faster, and even strengthens our hearts. Truly amazing.

So, these are some of the reasons why you might enlist a team of people to help you through this tough time—your partner, close friends, family members, a trained person, a stranger who

---

3   TEDGlobal, 2013. www.ted.com/talks/kelly_mcgonigal_how_to_make_stress_your_friend.
Accessed February 8, 2016.

is in the same situation, or even better, all of the above. Please don't try to go it alone—you will be fighting nature if you do.

You can be selective, though. If the people close to you don't seem to know how to give you the kind of support you need, by all means keep looking. Sometimes, a close friend or relative who means well will try the "pick yourself up by your bootstraps" approach. Not helpful. Let them know this is not what you need, tell them what you do need, and if that feedback doesn't work, there is surely another person in your life who is more open-minded and attuned.

Anne's close friends knew about the attack in her home, but she never told her children because she was determined not to burden them. Just this week, as I am putting the finishing touches on this section, "Anne" said these words: "I decided to speak to my boys after our last session and now I feel like a 1000-pound weight has been lifted. I had been feeling awful, and as soon as we spoke I felt euphoric, and even physically relieved." Oxytocin does that.

I had suggested that she might reconsider her decision to keep her sons in the dark about the attack. She raised them on her own. They happen to be responsible, well-adjusted young adults. I told her that she didn't have to go into any detail about the event if she preferred. What would help most is speaking honestly of the emotional impact. For example, "I felt helpless and terrified." She did, and reported back that she was blown away by their reaction. Not only did her sons react kindly, they actually said, "You haven't been yourself. We were worried. We want you to take care of yourself. We'll take it from here, Mom." Anne was never alone, but now she truly knows it. She can lean on her strong boys.

Anne's example gives us a glimpse of another reason, perhaps the best one, to confide in a loved one: their compassion opens the door to your own. If you have chosen well, your confidante will feel and express empathy. Most people find it quite natural to be compassionate to someone else's suffering. It is self-compassion that seems to be tricky.

If you are one of those people who feels shame, it is incredibly healing to experience, or "borrow", another's natural compassion for a time, until you can generate your own. Dr. Kirsten Neff, a psychologist who has made self-compassion her life's work, believes that self-compassion is very helpful to recover from trauma. Basically, it gives you what she calls the "calm courage" to ride the powerful waves of emotions that characterize PTSD.[4]

---

4   Kristen Neff, 2011, *Self-Compassion, The Proven Power of Being Kind to Yourself*, New York: Harper Collins. Her website, self-compassion.org, has a wealth of resources if you want to learn how to raise your level of self-compassion.

" The Mind is its own place, and in itself can **make** a Heaven of Hell, a Hell of Heaven. "

—John Milton

Part Three

PTSD Happens in the Brain

Now we turn the central purpose of this little book—to explain how PTSD happens. Bear with me, please—this is the longest section. I'll do my best to keep it light and interesting.

There is a good reason why the brain keeps replaying the traumatic event.

Edna Foa, a psychologist who has studied and treated victims of rape for decades, tells her patients that their experience was so disturbing, so "big," that it does not fit into what they already know about the world.

Perhaps it is like the expression "having something stuck in one's craw," like the bird in this picture. In any case, we think the memory keeps replaying as nightmares and flashbacks because the human mind doesn't like "unfinished business." It wants to finish processing the experience.

In other words, Dr. Foa sees PTSD as resulting from incomplete processing.

It all works as if there is a default system in the mind. When the person starts reacting to a reminder—a trigger—the brain seems to wake up to the fact that the traumatic event is still stuck. Still not finished processing the trauma? Here's a nightmare or a flashback. The intrusive symptoms have a purpose—to help process the event, or at least signal to the person that there is still something waiting in the queue.

Maybe over many years these symptoms would eventually do the job and help finish the processing, but why relive a painful experience in this distressing, uncontrolled, intrusive way, especially if there is quicker way?

People with PTSD describe feeling like there is some invisible force in their heads, randomly clicking a remote control and playing the film of the worst time in their life. And because it is their story and they are the heroes, they can't just watch the film. They have to step into the scene and re-enact it each time. It's truly crazy-making.

Dr. Foa's research has shown that in PTSD these intrusive efforts to re-process are not successful, and it is the person who ends up changing. Specifically, it is his or her view of the world and sense of safety that changes. The goal of therapy, then, is to facilitate the processing of the trauma, and the first step is to stop avoiding.

Why avoidance doesn't work

Before you can give up on avoidance, it is important that you understand why avoidance doesn't work.

Here is a metaphor to explain this. (I suppose you have noticed that I love metaphors. In fact, I collect them. As a French Canadian, I grew up with fables. They are helpful in my own life and with clients. They are stories that stick in the mind and plant a visual in your brain. James Geary's TED Talk *Metaphorically Speaking*[5] shows how the right metaphor can subtly influence behaviour. I chose mine to help boost your willingness to take action. I was so pleased to discover that there is a whole book dedicated to metaphors in therapy.[6])

---

5   https://www.ted.com/talks/james_geary_metaphorically_speaking. Accessed February 9, 2016.

6   Paul Blenkiron, 2010. *Stories and Analogies in Cognitive Behaviour Therapy*. Hoboken, NJ: Wiley-Blackwell.

Imagine a man pushing a snowball (the problem) in front of him on the road. In the short term, this strategy of avoidance lets the individual take a few more steps, but the snowball remains on the road, gathering up more snow. The person would do better to stop, face the problem, and chip at the packed snowball bit by bit until the road ahead was clear.

Or if you prefer, you could think of a cupboard where books were thrown into in a hurry. The door will not close properly and the books fall out unpredictably.

To avoid the falling books, it is natural to stay away, but the longer you put off cleaning the cupboard, the more hazardous it becomes.

One day you say, "Enough is enough." Each book has to be examined and put in its proper place on the right shelf. Once this is done, the door will close and the books—the memories—will be within reach when you decide you want to look at them.

So PTSD is a problem with the human mind's way of processing trauma. To understand it and gain some control over it it is important to know something about how it works.

In a nutshell, we have inherited an old brain, one that we share with animals, and a beautiful new, evolved brain. The new one basically sits on top of the old one. In fact, it grew a bit like a house does—basement, ground floor, first storey. This means that our brain does not function like a computer, but more like an orchestra, or a well-practiced ensemble cast.

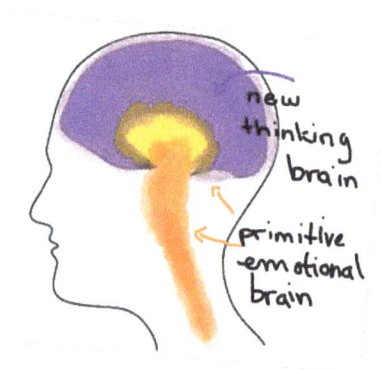

And an emergency might be the only time one notices that it is not always a smooth performance. Why? Because the old brain is set up to automatically override the new brain whenever we are in danger. Psychologist Daniel Goleman actually calls it an "emotional hijacking."[7]

As you instinctively jump on the sidewalk just in time to avoid a speeding truck, you might become aware that there are in fact two major systems, or routes, or levels, of information processing—an automatic one and a deliberate, or conscious one. You didn't "decide" to jump in the way that word usually means, like when you "decided" to take this street rather than that one, or pick up some bread on the way home. Your thinking brain was hijacked—it is an apt metaphor. (I wish I came up with it.)

When the threat system fires up, it does so automatically. Because it is part of the "old brain" it is not under direct control. Its product, the stress response, is a reflex programmed by evolution that kicks in when we are under threat.

Even though you don't control it directly, understanding how the stress response works can give you some indirect influence over it and prevent its effects from turning harmful or becoming chronic. At the very least, it can discourage you from blaming yourself when there is a "glitch." So let's look at the two levels, or routes, mentioned earlier.

---

7   Daniel Goleman, 1995. *Emotional Intelligence*. New York: Bantam Books.

The two levels of information processing

In these pages I will refer to these two levels as routes to emphasize that information is processed along two different channels. I could talk about brain structures but that gets tricky, so let's stick to function.

I will call them the high and low routes, because as I said, the brain is set up roughly that way. I will use a turtle to represent the much slower high route, and a rabbit to represent the faster low route—like in the fable, but for other reasons too.

The high route represents the thinking level of processing, and will appear in green.

The low route represents the emotional / physiological level of processing. Its colour will be red. I will keep these colours very consistent throughout the book.

When you encounter a threat, the brain becomes aware of it in the same way as it would any other outside event—through your senses. One or more of the five senses inform the mind of the potential danger. I chose a cartoon bomb to symbolize the trauma event or events.

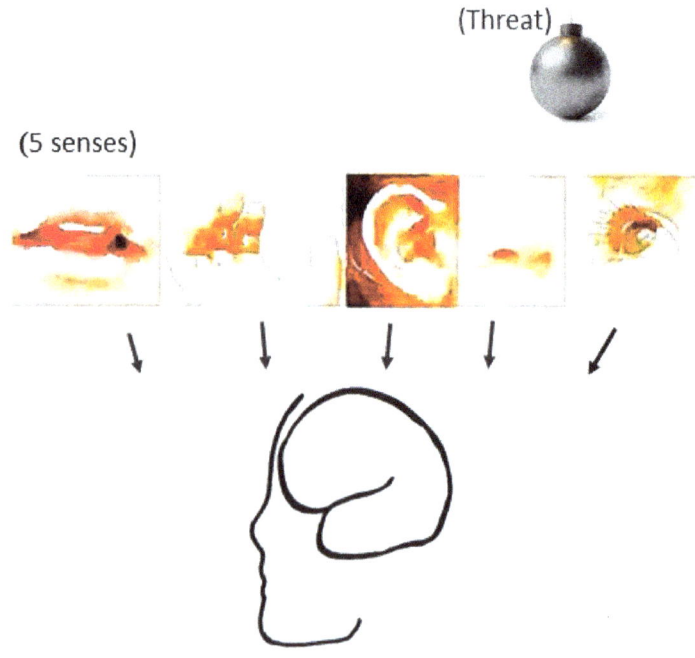

(Threat)

(5 senses)

The normal stress response: the **high** route and the **low** route

This information makes its way along different paths in the brain in order to be processed, or understood.

Right away, the path branches off into the high route and the low route. The information about the threat follows both of these routes simultaneously, but at very different speeds.

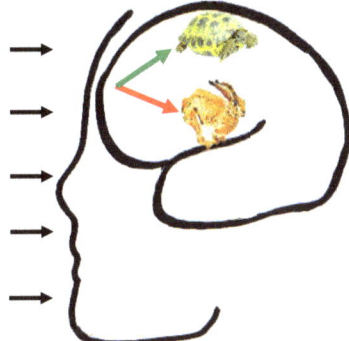

As we saw earlier, the high route leads to the thinking level, or the level of conscious awareness. It leads to a uniquely human understanding of the situation, and to a planned response.

In the meantime, the low route (the automatic, primitive system we share with animals) comes to an almost immediate decision about whether the fear network needs to engage. It is the shortcut, the express route.

So, both routes lead to independent "appraisals," or evaluations, of the threat, even if the person is only consciously aware of the high route process.

An experience of Martin's in Bosnia gives a good example of this two-part process. As he is driving along a road, a boy jumps in front of the vehicle, aiming a machine-gun straight at him and his buddies. With his heart pounding, and guided by the "reflexes" provided by his low route, he aims the truck in the boy's direction, ready to run him over if necessary.

At the last minute, he realizes that the "gun" is in fact a branch.

If there had been real danger, the low route might have saved Martin's life and that of his passengers. As it turned out, the processing done by his high route saved the day by checking his first appraisal and intercepting the actions based on the crude plan of his low route.

So, when the normal stress response is working properly, as in this example, the two types of interpretation are complementary and in synch. The processing done by one always lags behind the other, but the high and low routes do converge in the end.

The two separate appraisals to which they lead are both influenced by past experiences. It is as if the information about the threat is being "filtered" by past experiences.

The filter of past experiences

The filter of past experiences represents a broad set of factors that affect how we handle events. Its first job in a potentially dangerous situation is to help determine if the brain's emergency response network should be activated.

In many ways, this filter represents learning and memory, but inherited things like gender and temperament play a part as well. Past experiences that relate to the current threatening situation shape the filter, which will be represented in blue.

- ← temperament, predispositions
- ← memories
- ← experience
- ← training

The filter can prepare the individual to deal effectively with a specific threat. For example, if I were trained as a bomb expert, that would presumably help me choose a strategy from a broader set of choices than the average person may have.

The filter can also sensitize. For example, a soldier who, on a previous tour, had seen people who had been maimed by a bomb might have a stronger emotional reaction.

Both the preparedness and the sensitization parts of the filter are flexible. To do its job, the filter must always be ready to accommodate new experiences.

Of course, there is no such structure in the brain. The filter is just one more metaphor, used to illustrate the factors that influence the mind's decisions.

Perhaps some readers will want to see a more realistic picture of the brain, showing structure rather than function. Here's a really simple one that has all the essentials you need to understand PTSD. The cortex, and particularly the frontal cortex is where

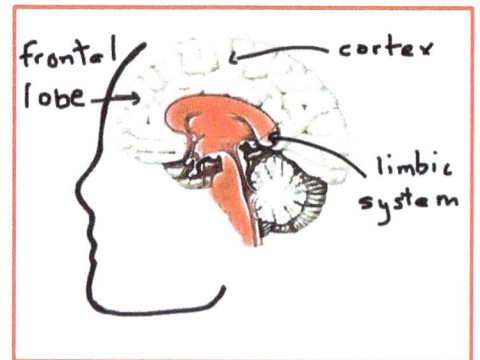

high level thinking and planning take place. The limbic system is the emotional brain, where the low route travels.

Summary picture 1: The normal stress response

The following summary picture, the first of three, illustrates the workings of the normal stress response, pulling together all of the elements we have just seen. It reads from left to right. Notice that a dotted line divides the high and low levels, or the conscious and unconscious levels. The line also goes right through the filter, to indicate that it, too, has both a conscious and an unconscious level.

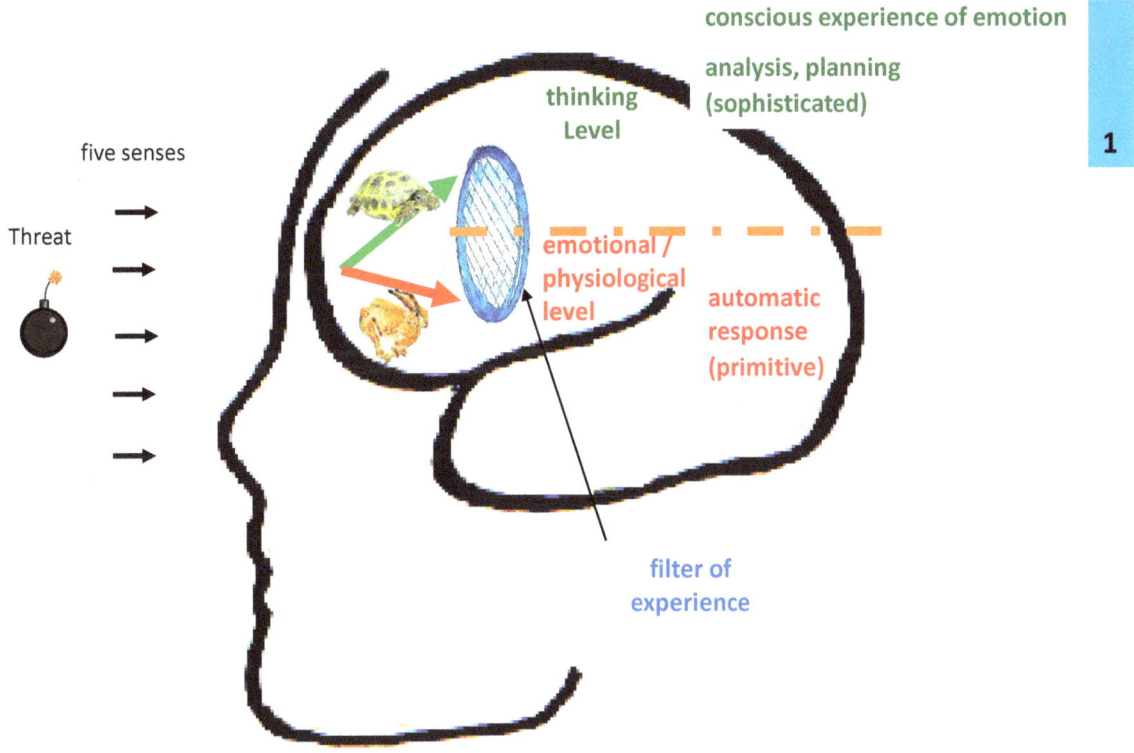

Now let's look more closely at this process. As the information about the threat travels down the high and low routes in the first response phase, both levels of processing are active.

The high route is the one of which we are most clearly aware. As a potentially dangerous situation is encountered, this thinking route leads to many questions, which in turn leads to making conscious choices and plans.

"Oh-oh, how dangerous is this?"
"What do I know about this danger?
"What is my best bet, here:
  retreat, or do something?"

Meanwhile, the low route has independently and almost instantly come to its own decision about the seriousness of this threat and set the ball rolling based on preliminary impressions. As we have seen, the evolution and design of the low route stress response system needs very little information or time to respond during emergencies. This rapid response system works the same way for an animal facing a predator, a prehistoric man facing a bear, or a shy, modern-day human facing a crowd.

To begin the chain of events of the low route, the alarm is sounded—this is done by increasing the brain's level of arousal.

Specialized structures in the brain quickly determine if the threat is serious or not. The amygdala has been getting a lot of press lately as the "star" of the brain's fear network. (It got its name because of its oval shape: "amygdala" comes from the Greek word for almond.)

As you can see in the picture, there are two amygdalae deep inside the limbic brain —one on either side. They are a crucial part of the circuit that enables our brains to detect and respond to threats of any kind.

The amygdala is often portrayed as the fear centre of the brain, as if the amygdala were working alone, but, not surprisingly, it turns out not to be the case.[8] The brain is complicated—it really does work as an ensemble cast.

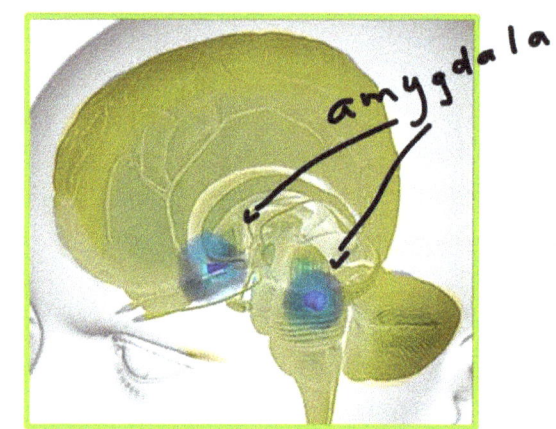

Getting back to our story, if the brain decides that the threat is not serious, the arousal level quickly returns to normal and the high level stays in control. If it deems the threat serious, the mind moves from yellow to red alert, which means:

---

8   *How Emotions Are Made: The New Science Of The Mind And Brain* (Sept. 2016. Boston, MA: Houghton Mifflin Harcourt) by neuroscientist Dr. Lisa Feldman Barrett shows that emotions do not have a distinct pattern in the brain and are not simple neural entities.

1. Other emotions are numbed.

2. Attention is enhanced and is focused solely on the perceived danger.

3. All body systems are ready and on standby for:

fight

freeze

flight

Some animals are more adept at one response than another. As a rule, birds choose flight (literally), animals with good camouflage freeze, and felines fight. Humans, thanks to a uniquely developed, conscious high route process, are able to choose the best course of action based on logic. Or habits. Or training. Or temperament. It is undeniable that some of us are more likely to fight than others, based on what happens to be in our filters.

Incidentally, PTSD patients often second-guess what they did at the time of the trauma. For example, if they ran, they wish they had fought, and vice versa.

Anne blames herself for not hitting her assailant over the head with something handy like a lamp when she had the chance. A therapist would caution her about the perils of "Monday morning quarterbacking." His first question would be, "What experience do you have with fighting off an attacker? Do you have training in self-defence?" Another way of asking, "Is that response even in your filter, Anne?"

In order to prepare the body for any course of action, heart rate, blood pressure, breathing rate, and sweat production all increase. At this point on the low route, the body is simply saying, "all systems are go."

A secondary effect of this increased arousal is that memory is enhanced by the narrowly focused attention, and by the "glue" provided by the strong emotions associated with high arousal. Evolution has placed the memory and emotional circuits of the brain close together for good reason. This effect—enhanced memory at times of stress—has been called flash-bulb memory.

The memory for the experience is then virtually burned into the filter, becoming part of it. This effect ensures that whenever this particular individual or animal faces a similar situation, anything learned on a past occasion will be quickly available in a new situation.

Joseph LeDoux, a brain scientist who has done pioneering research on emotions and who discovered the role of the amygdala in fear, writes that the human brain's power to form memories of dangerous situations, retain them indefinitely, and call them up automatically when similar situations arise, is one of its most efficient functions. [9] However, he also sees it as a luxury with a high price tag. If you have PTSD, or know someone who does, you know why.

---

9 *   Joseph LeDoux, 1998. *The Emotional Brain: the Mysterious Underpinnings of Emotional Life*, New York: Simon and Shuster.

Summary picture 2: Early reaction to trauma

The second summary picture that follows shows the workings of the normal stress response. It goes through the chain of events on the low route step by step.

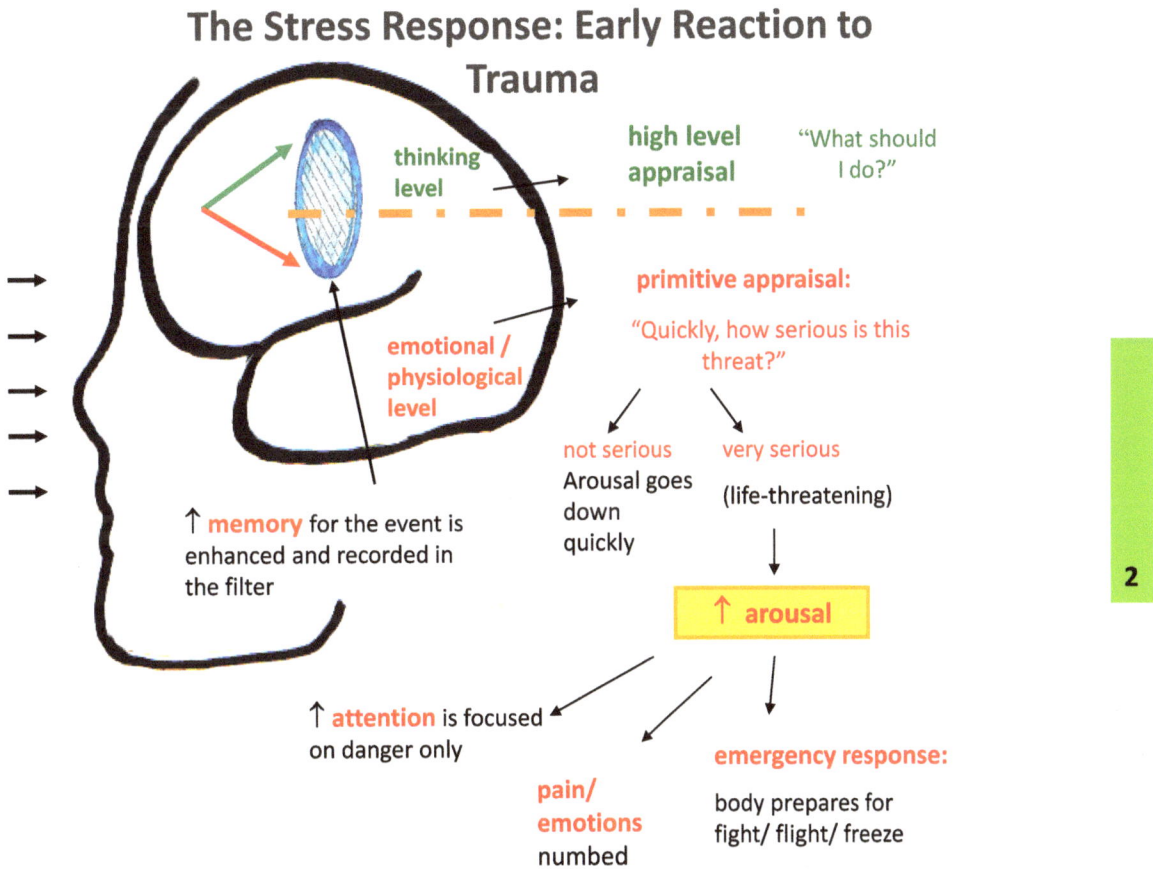

The Stress Response: Early Reaction to Trauma

thinking level

high level appraisal

"What should I do?"

primitive appraisal:

"Quickly, how serious is this threat?"

emotional / physiological level

↑ memory for the event is enhanced and recorded in the filter

not serious
Arousal goes down quickly

very serious
(life-threatening)

↑ arousal

↑ attention is focused on danger only

pain/ emotions numbed

emergency response:
body prepares for fight/ flight/ freeze

Serious stress can make us fall back into a mode of operation in which we react instead of thinking. The low process is the default option: it bypasses or overrides the rational process at times of emergency, allowing evolution to do the thinking when time is of the essence.

The incredibly efficient design of the stress response saves lives. If evolution had allowed the new thinking level to stay in control in all situations, humankind would probably be extinct as there would no longer be a survival instinct.

But when it kicks in at a time when there is no emergency, it does more harm than good. With PTSD, this incredibly efficient stress response or emergency system becomes stuck. In effect, the low route does not return to normal after the crisis is over, as it is supposed to. PTSD therefore starts off as a problem with the low route.

It is as if the filter has been damaged, or sensitized by the trauma. The part below consciousness has been too effective, recording all of the details so efficiently that any one of them, important or trivial, can automatically re-trigger the whole chain of brain events along the low route.

It works like this: one of the senses brings in an external reminder of the trauma. For instance, the ordinary smell of smoke might remind a soldier of a bomb he faced in the past. The sensitized filter sends this information at lightning speed down the low route.

This is where the brain's fear network comes into play. As we saw a few pages ago, the brain has a very cool design feature that specializes in the assessment of danger. Evolution has programmed this network to favour speed over accuracy. It operates like an adaptable, natural alarm system pre-programmed by evolution.

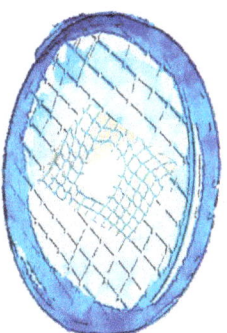

Speed and survival are closely linked, because it is always preferable to have false alarms than it is to have even a single dead animal.

In a world where the alternative is being eaten, jumping the gun makes sense from an evolutionary perspective. In nature, it pays to have a system that says, "That movement in the trees over there—don't waste any time checking it out. Run! It's a predator."

So, in PTSD, the oversensitive amygdala system, working on this "better safe than sorry" principle, routinely jumps to the wrong conclusion, and sets off the "red alert" arousal sequence. It has learned to associate the trigger—sound, smell, sight, or memory—with life-threatening stress.

Hyper-vigilance is too much of a good thing.

The amygdala system acts like a sentinel that is always alert, even during sleep. It reacts to information coming from the senses long before the cortex is able to grasp what is happening. If the sentinel determines that the threat is serious, it prepares and propels us to take life-saving action.

The problem is that it calls "911" without waiting to get all of the information. It does this at the best of times, but in PTSD, it is not just vigilant, it is hyper-vigilant. The experience of Nicholas, the first responder who had a panic attack in the movie theatre, is a clear example of this. He is in no danger, and his cortex knows it, but his amygdala system, triggered by a dramatization of a terrible accident, has no way of appreciating this.

The alarm system of a house works on the same principle. It gets triggered when the window breaks, whether it is due to a branch falling or because a robber just smashed it. It is not its job to discriminate between the wind and the robber. We need a much more evolved brain region to do this type of sophisticated discrimination.

In PTSD, there is a new problem, however. The alarm system of the "house" has gotten stuck on high somehow. It now reacts to the squirrel on the roof, not just to shattered glass. That oversensitivity may seem protective at first glance. Too many veterans I know feel it is perfectly normal to have a baseball bat in every room or to sleep with a knife under their pillow.

In actual fact, hyper-vigilance can mean trading one risk for another, like in the story of little boy who cried wolf, or in heartbreaking friendly fire events. Enough said.

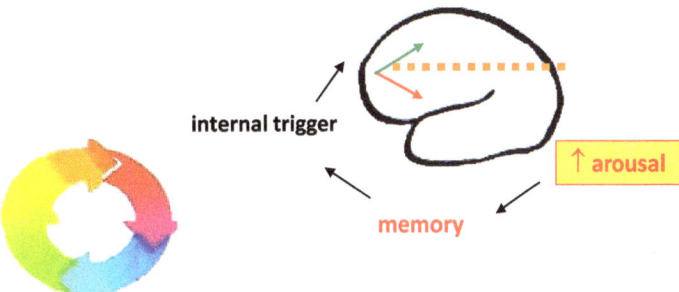

internal trigger

↑ arousal

memory

Once the system gets stuck in this way, either because of one big alert or a number of smaller ones, a series of things start happening:

- All emotions become numbed, including pleasurable ones, like affection.
- The body, stuck in fight/flight/freeze, cannot relax or sleep efficiently.
- Moods become irritable and temper is harder to control.
- Attention is disrupted, which interferes with work and pastimes.
- Because the memory systems of the brain are closely associated with our emotional systems, memory then connects the heightened arousal state with trauma, triggering unwanted memories, nightmares, and flashbacks - the re-experiencing, or intrusive symptoms.
- The cycle begins again, this time with an internal cue or trigger. (This is the truly "vicious" part of the cycle.)

N.B. In extreme, prolonged arousal, the exact opposite effect can occur: memory can break down due to the effects of different stress hormones. So some things are remembered vividly, while others never even registered. This means that there is no point in worrying or beating yourself up about gaps in memory if you have some.

Anne, Martin, and Nicholas all find, to their dismay, that their symptoms seem to get worse on the days when they have spoken to someone about the incident, such as the police or a friend, or after a bad nightmare.

The memory of the trauma (an internal trigger) is enough to start the whole process again. No wonder they all want to stay away from the reminders, and avoid talking about the trauma. Avoidance makes perfect sense, logically. But the problem is that this logic does not work here.

Summary picture 3: Chronic PTSD

The third summary picture puts it all together. It is different and more complicated because it shows what happens to the two routes of the normal stress response when someone develops PTSD.

It shows the stress response once it has become stuck and stopped being functional. Notice the yellow boxes representing the four key groups of PTSD symptoms. Their ink colour tells you at a glance to which route they belong.

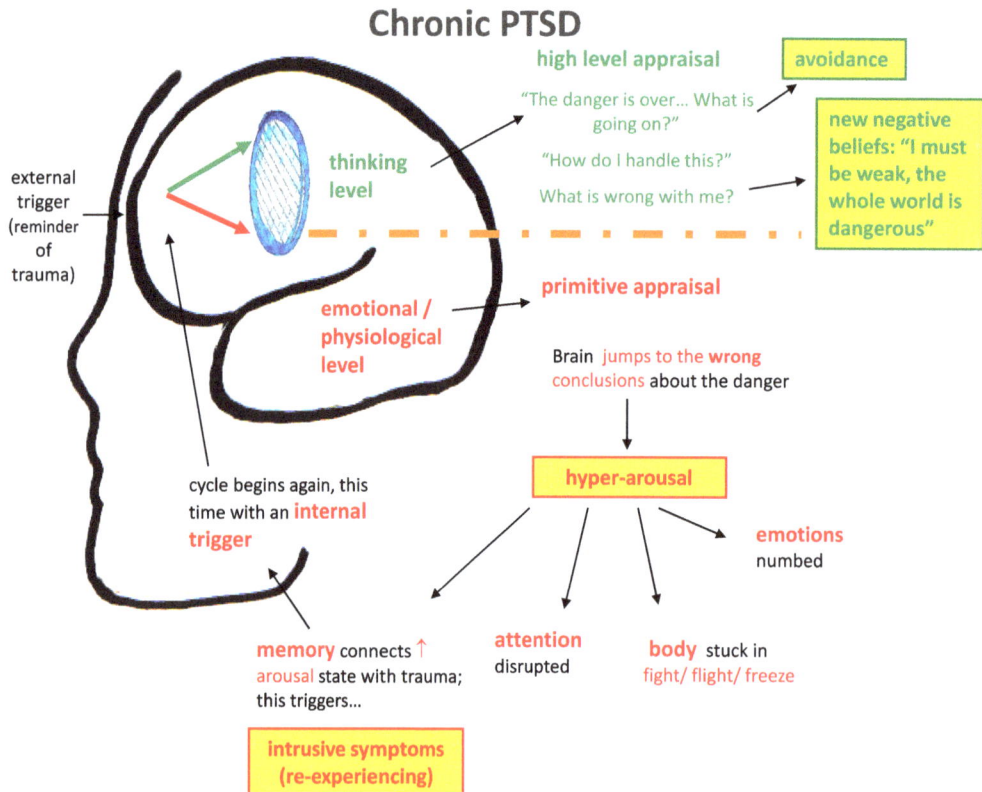

We have now seen that two out of the four symptoms central to PTSD (re-experiencing and hyper-arousal) are problems associated with the low route. They are the results of a simple kind of learning.

The third group of symptoms of PTSD is avoidance. This is a high route problem, and as you would expect, represents a more sophisticated kind of learning, or "conditioning".

To understand avoidance, and also the fourth and last cluster of symptoms, we must now turn our attention to the high route.

The high route in PTSD

Keep in mind that all of the activity of the low route goes on below the dotted line, and at speeds that the turtle-like thinking level can never match. This means that the high level will often become aware of powerful emotional and physical reactions before it has a chance to figure out what is causing the reaction.

To say the least, this is an unsettling experience for the thinking level, which is used to being in control. It is the job of the high route to make sense out of things, so questions will naturally arise.

Given the split between the two levels of processing, and given that emergency responses are very strong reactions, it is not surprising that PTSD sufferers secretly wonder if they are going crazy.

Not only are you having physical and emotional reactions over which you have no control, but you may even behave in ways that you know are not rational.

For example, a woman who was attacked in an elevator starts to take the stairs all the time, even for twenty flights.

Another example: a man who was in a fire avoids campfires at first. Later, he makes excuses not to use the fireplace at home. Eventually, he cannot light his barbecue or tolerate birthday candles. He may not even know why.

These behaviours are examples of avoidance. Imagine that you have strange symptoms—dizziness, nightmares, sweating, heart palpitations—each time you cross a certain wobbly bridge, give blood, or eat a papaya. Wouldn't you steer clear of these things? Of course you would.

Avoiding the triggers as much as possible is the first thing anybody tries. The PTSD sufferer, even without necessarily knowing what is going on, quickly learns to avoid smells, sights, sounds, and even topics of conversation that precede intrusive symptoms. Crowds, confined spaces, noisy places, and malls are part of many people's list of things to avoid, but there are situations and things specific to each individual.

Anne crosses the street whenever she sees people who look anything like the man who broke into her home. She might react to someone wearing the same colour cap, or a similar scent, even if that makes no apparent sense.

Martin, the soldier, never watches the news and leaves the room whenever he hears a child in distress.

For his part, Nicholas was more fortunate. He had friends with PTSD so he sought help soon after he left the movie theatre. Avoidance never became a pattern for him. He did not develop full-blown PTSD.

The problem with avoidance is this: it is an excellent short-term solution, addictive even, because the relief is immediate. But it is a terrible long-term solution because it typically makes the problem worse. Experiments with cats have shown that avoidance is extremely hard to unlearn. If a cat hears a buzzer just before its paws receive an electric shock, and it realizes that it can avoid the shock by jumping over a wall, it doesn't take long for it to learn to jump each time the buzzer sounds. The animal does not let itself find out if it is safe to stay put; long after the shock has stopped, it continues to jump as soon as it hears the buzzer. The brain's SOP (standard operating procedure) is "better safe than sorry."

If anything, humans are even more efficient learners than cats. This is why irrational fears such as the fear of elevators or dogs seem unreasonable, even to the sufferer, yet most people can understand how hard they must be to overcome because most of us have felt that type of fear before.

Why PTSD seems to wax and wane

The tricky thing is that avoidance is more than just ineffective. It actually seems to work as a motor that makes PTSD symptoms swing like a pendulum between two extremes: numbing and re-experiencing. It certainly does seem that symptoms go through more disruptive and then quieter phases (Horowitz).[10]

Here is a picture to illustrate this metaphor.

---

10   Mardi J. Horowitz, 2011, *Stress Response Syndromes: PTSD Grief, Adjustment* , and *Dissociative Disorders, 5th edition*, Jason Aronson Inc., 2011

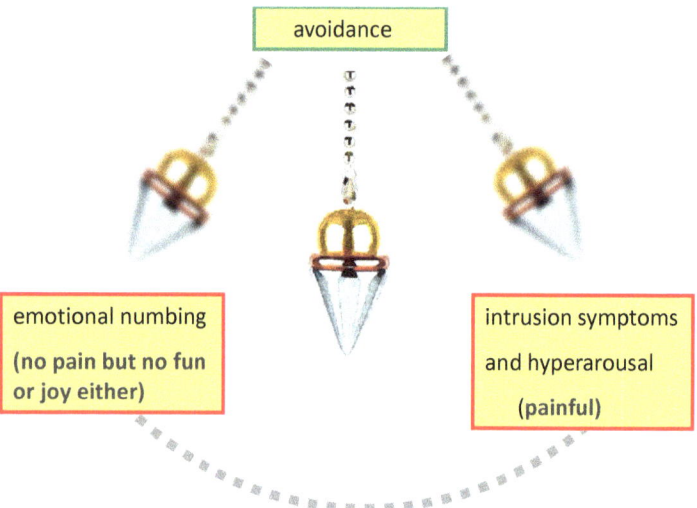

Avoidance seems to make the pendulum swing towards the numb side, but then with the momentum it swings back to the re-experiencing side. The swinging gets more rapid and the two "red" symptoms get stronger. At first the person thinks they are controlling the symptoms. Before long, it's the opposite—they feel out of control.

Recovery begins by carefully phasing out avoidance. Without avoidance, the other symptoms still swing for a good while. In fact, they increase at first. (I'm sorry.) Then, over time, they decrease and fade. For some lucky few, they actually disappear.

To have a good idea of how exposure and avoidance differ, imagine leaving a darkened cinema and stepping out into the bright sunlight. You are blinded; it is quite painful. But you know what this is and you are not worried. Going back inside would immediately put an end to the pain, but this strategy of avoidance does not cross your mind. You know that if you are patient the feeling will pass. You choose exposure.

Now, let's turn to the last group of symptoms, negative changes in thoughts and moods.

Here's a good question. The Cognitive Behavioural Therapy school of psychology says that thoughts lead to feelings, not events themselves. But we have just finished seeing that the low route leads to strong emotions indeed, based on an appraisal that involves virtually no thinking. How does that work?

The emotions of the high and low routes are different

The low route leads to a narrow set of basic emotions like fear and anger, which are strong, natural feelings. Animals actually have similar emotions.

In contrast, the high route leads to a much broader range of emotions. They are more complex, human, and individual, such as guilt, shame, distrust, pity, self-hatred, resentment, and disillusionment.

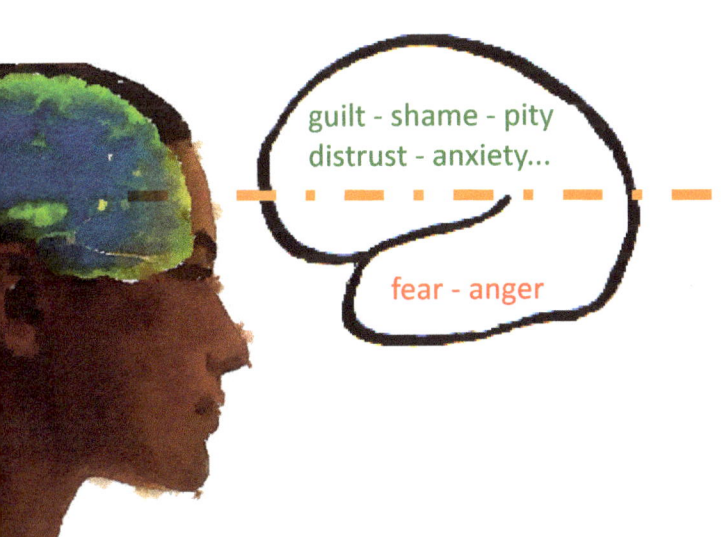

guilt - shame - pity
distrust - anxiety...

fear - anger

In PTSD, these second-level emotions are not as closely tied to the traumatic event. They follow interpretations, or "appraisals" that try to make sense out of the event or its aftermath.

For example, almost anyone would feel fear if they saw a gun pointed at them or if they were raped, but only some people would feel shame afterwards.

To understand why a particular emotion like shame arose in this person in this instance, we would have to know the meaning of what happened for them—or, more simply, what they say to themselves—what does their self-talk sound like?

For example, "I should have fought harder," or "I should have seen it coming," or "I had no business being in that neighbourhood at night in the first place."

Any of these thoughts would lead a person to feel responsible for what happened, or ashamed. There may be some validity to what they are thinking, perhaps more than a grain of truth. But if you think about it, these conclusions are too general to be accurate. The victim of a crime isn't the one who will be arrested; the perpetrator goes to jail, the victim goes home.

Here is another example: Sam and Marie, two police officers, are called to the scene of a car accident. Two passengers die en route to the hospital, but the driver is saved thanks to their skill and quick thinking.

Both officers feel badly of course, but Sam takes comfort in the thought that he helped to save a life, while Marie feels terribly guilty that she did not arrive in time to save the others.

As she talks it over with Sam, it occurs to her that she has overlooked something important: the road conditions were treacherous. Come to think of it, the weather was the reason for the accident. Trying to get to the scene any faster would have been reckless. This changes her thinking to: "Actually, I guess I did everything I could, it was just not possible to save them all in the circumstances." She is still sad, but her guilt dissipates.

The example of Sam and Marie shows how thoughts can lead to emotions. Here are other examples of thoughts that often complicate a reaction to traumatic events:

"This is not fair." (anger)

"I will never recover from this." (discouragement)

"People cannot be trusted." (anxiety, distrust)

"I'd never be in this mess if it wasn't for…." (resentment)

For Dr. Foa and her colleagues, people who experience a trauma and go on to develop PTSD incorporate the experience by drawing new conclusions (or solidifying old ones) and adopting beliefs along two themes:

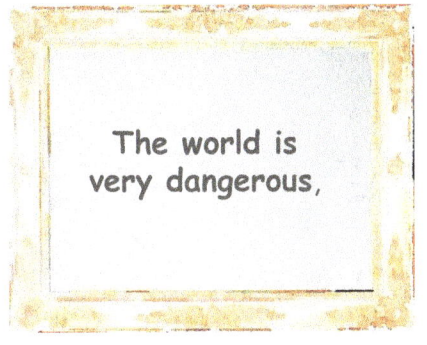

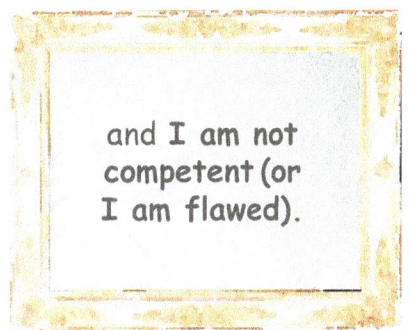

Having thoughts along these lines is understandable for someone who has undergone a traumatic experience. Anne's family understands that she sees her home as unsafe at night since the attack.

However, the problem is that these thoughts are way too general. They are no longer tied to specific situations, but have become rigid, negative beliefs—similar to a prejudice. Her home is no less safe than it was prior to the break-in. In fact, it is probably safer: she put extra security measures in place and you can be sure that she never forgets to set the alarm or lock her doors.

Such beliefs are no longer products of case-by-case, flexible, high route processing—it is as if they have become part of a filter that makes decisions speedier, but at a cost.

The solution is to break the thinking habits, get back to flexibility. This is easier said than done, of course.

Now, let's talk about therapy.

"When you are going through hell, keep going."

—Winston Churchill

Part Four

How Therapy Works

Two main routes for recovery

Most therapies work at one level more directly than the other. Some medications, for example, primarily affect the low route. Some therapies involve both routes at once, reasoning that a two-fold approach is more likely to be successful.

You may remember that my promise to you was to get you through the psycho-education phase of therapy, which you can certainly count as a very important first step. But afterwards, you really have to go through that door.

We can't get into the pros and cons of each good therapy approach in these pages, but I can give you a few examples to give you a feel for what lies ahead, and illustrate how the two levels of processing come into play.

Cognitive-Behavioural Therapy

Cognitive-Behavioural Therapy (CBT) is probably the therapy that is the most widely used to treat PTSD because it has excellent scientific support. It travels both routes.

The cognitive strategies involve the high route. Any overly general, negative beliefs are drawn into the light so they can be looked at, and if need be, tested and challenged. As we saw earlier, beliefs are a problem when they are not just negative, but also too rigidly held. When Sam helped Marie think about the rescue in a different way, he was being a good cognitive therapist.

When Anne's therapist pointed out that it would have been pretty hard for her to fight off her assailant when he had the element of surprise and she had no training in self-defence he was using a cognitive approach to address her shame. It worked. Once they were able to entertain a more flexible, balanced point of view, Marie and Anne started to feel better. The feelings attached to the old thought patterns decreased. Often, they actually dissolve.

A behavioural approach challenges beliefs through experience and action instead of talk. It facilitates a dialogue between the emotional and rational systems. This approach challenges the strategy of avoidance very directly, in effect stopping the "motor" for the pendulum.

Exposure: the countermeasure

Exposure is the opposite of avoidance. It is one of the most powerful strategies to over-come PTSD available. Your therapist encourages you to face the situations that you have been avoiding in real life (like sitting by a fire at a safe distance) or in memory (by reading your story every day for a set period of time). You take controlled, manageable steps; the fear decreases day by day, and eventually it loses its grip.

Now, this does not mean forgetting. The memory remains—evolution has seen to it that animals and humans don't forget any life lesson associated with survival. But the memory can be separated from hot emotion, or "deactivated," and that makes all the difference.

Prolonged exposure (PE) works like this. First, you practice techniques like deep breathing or meditation to calm the low route hyper-arousal, and create, or activate, "self-soothing" circuits in your brain. (No, taking substances like alcohol, benzos or cannabis to relax does not count, because the whole idea is for you to set down new tracks in your brain that enable you to calm yourself on your own at will. It does take a few weeks or more of dedi-cated practice but is totally possible if you set your mind to it.)

Then, your therapist will ask you to tell your trauma story, and support you while you do so. She will encourage you to remember each event, one at a time, as vividly as possible, calling upon all your senses. In doing so, your brain's emergency system is triggered in the safety of the therapist's office.

Reliving the story in therapy is by no means easy but it feels very different than a flashback: with exposure, you take command of the remote control. The film starts when you press "play" and stops when you press "stop."

Did you ever watch a horror movie so many times that the monster no longer seemed frightening, and you didn't forget that you were watching a movie?

With exposure, the same thing happens with your own script. It starts to feel like a film that you are watching, as opposed to living it for real.

Dr. Foa calls this "having one foot in the past, and one foot in the present," because each time you deliberately take out the film of the trauma story and let it play to the end, it changes a little bit. Each time, it seems to get a nice "coating" of the present, like when you look around the room to take a break from the action on the TV screen and remind yourself, "It's only a movie."

As you play the story voluntarily, your emotional level is able, little by little, to absorb the safety of the current situation, and truly grasp that the story is not actually happening. It is just that—a story, a memory—and as unpleasant as they can be, memories carry no danger.

The animal part of the brain does not comprehend words; it has to be shown that there is no danger. A cat that has been mistreated by its previous owner will be reassured only over time, through experience.

Once the trauma is truly "processed" in this way, the fear fades and even dissipates. Maybe the filter is stitched, or the tortoise and the hare work in tandem again to reach the finish line. Or the two roads merge smoothly like they are meant to. Anyway, emotions stop their hijacking. Thinking gets back in the driver's seat—at least until the next real emergency. (Six metaphors in five sentences; this could be a record.)

Now you understand PTSD. Thank you for staying with this.

Are you still hesitating to get help, not quite convinced that avoidance isn't the best way after all?

If so, well, you are certainly not alone. It is very difficult to go against such strong instincts. After all, in the physical world, avoidance works. You don't put your hand on a hot stove twice. It's hard to grasp that the brain works differently.[11]

---

11   This, by the way, is the premise of a school of therapy called Acceptance and Commitment Therapy. It is not just for PTSD, but certainly has a lot to offer to the treatment of PTSD. These people might like metaphors even more than I do. The first ACT book to read is: Stephen Hayes, 2011. *The Process and Practice of Mindful Change*. New York: Guilford Press.

This is a little diagram I drew for Robert, a patient who, like almost everyone I meet with PTSD, was determined to be the exception to the rule—the one guy who succeeds in making avoidance work. He was sticking to the left side of the picture, certain that this strategy was keeping him safe.

Really, though, it was keeping him miserable.

He had yet to learn that pain and suffering are two related but different things. Pain is part and parcel of the human condition, as inevitable as the seasons, but also fleeting: this too shall pass. Suffering is optional. It is a byproduct of the efforts not to feel, the efforts to deny, repress, push aside the pain. It is a paradox: the more we fight, the longer we suffer. It took a very long time, years, to convince Robert of this.

With time, he understood that he had to go through the first doorway, from "avoid" to "face," if he wanted to get better. When he did, each time he read the story of his trauma (the detailed account of an awful day in Afghanistan), his anxiety felt like a big menacing wave that was going to engulf him. It didn't. Over many days and many readings, the waves got smaller and smaller, until one day he discovered they had stopped. He stepped through the next doorway to "live" without even realizing it. I saw him that week. It was a different man who walked into my office. He looked somehow taller, his gait more fluid, and his face had a peaceful expression that was wonderful to behold.

"Feelings come and go like clouds in a windy sky. Conscious breathing " is my anchor.

—Thich Nhat Hanh

(time)

Before closing this book, here is one last metaphor to nudge you in the direction of facing your demons rather than trying to outrun them. In the image above, the man can safely stare down the gargoyle. How come?

Because the precipice represents time. No beast, no matter how powerful, can leap over time. The trauma is over—it can never return. Reliving it in your mind can never come close to living it for real, and you have already done that, and survived. Your memories of trauma may be painful but they can no longer harm you. Face them and they will lose their power over you.

I hope that this little book and its pictures and metaphors has helped you gain a better understanding of PTSD so you can fully grasp why it truly is not your fault, that you are not alone, that PTSD is a brain thing, and that when you trade avoidance for exposure, your recovery begins.

Having a better understanding of how our old and new minds react to trauma and sometimes get stuck will help you let go of shame, seek out support and treatment, resolve to face your experiences, and above all, find hope.

Bon courage, be well, don't give up, and may the roads rise up to meet you.

"The best way out is always through."

—Robert Frost

Afterword

If you think you may be suffering from some of the symptoms of PTSD, please do not delay in seeking professional attention. If you think you see them in a friend or partner or colleague or family member, whatever you do, please do not stay silent. There is no reason or basis for shame. Trauma is part of the human experience.

The first step is diagnosis, and its importance cannot be overstated. Don't try to diagnose yourself or let an untrained person take a guess! One of the biggest mistakes is when people equate a distressing event with trauma and its negative effects, assuming a direct cause and effect relationship: "You survived a plane crash (or a tsunami, or 911, or Afghanistan, or the Lac Megantic catastrophe, or decades of police work)? You must have PTSD." Many of the symptoms of PTSD resemble those of other conditions. Trauma, like beauty, is a subjective experience, and there are many ways to react to a potentially traumatic event, so please keep an open mind.

For a diagnostic assessment, the first stop is your family doctor, who will refer you or your loved one to a psychiatrist or psychologist registered in your province. These are the two professions who can diagnose in Canada. Other professions can treat once the diagnosis is made, especially in clinic settings. Some clinicians are in specialized clinics, some work on their own. If your family doctor does not know someone who has good experience with PTSD, you can contact the psychology and psychiatry departments of universities and hospitals in your area or in large urban centres. They will usually be able to provide you with a list of clinicians in your area who can assess and treat PTSD. Do you happen to know anyone who has been in treatment for this condition or a similar one? Asking people you respect for recommendations is a tried and true approach.

Keep in mind that the clinician who makes the diagnosis is not necessarily the one who will become your therapist. This first clinician should clarify the limits of his role from the outset and if he is not able to take on the therapy role, he will help you select and transfer to your therapist, the one who will guide you through the steps to recovery. Before moving on, make sure you truly understand what the first clinician thinks the diagnosis is and what it means for you. Even if it is PTSD, it is not unusual to have other "side" diagnoses like depression or substance abuse or traits like perfectionism that colour the picture and impact the therapy.

Credentials and experience are very important, but "fit" matters just as much. Please, do not stop until you have found someone with whom you feel comfortable and you feel you can trust. If you can't trust fully, it will be hard to open up, and if you cannot be honest with your therapist, the therapy just won't work.

Martha Beck, life coach and author, compares choosing a therapist to dating rather than shopping, and I can see her point. For this reason I suggest treating the first session as a trial. In fact, many therapists make a point of stating this explicitly when meeting patients for the first time. By all means, inquire if you might turn the table on the therapist a bit to ask the questions that are important to you and make sure you both understand each other's expectations. For example, if you are a soldier or police officer, you might want to know if your therapist knows about that world. For some clients, this knowledge of their specific context is important; for others, it isn't. In general, if something matters to you, then it matters, period.

You know me by now. You won't be surprised to read that I would listen carefully to the therapist's metaphors about PTSD. If she says that it is like an amputation or a meteor hitting the earth creating a crater that can never be filled (oh how I wish these examples were made-up), personally I would keep looking, or at least ask a lot of questions about hope. Hope is an essential ingredient for change, and therapists have to feel and express it, especially at the beginning when the client has difficulty feeling it herself.

If after this first hour, you are uneasy about anything, especially if you are not sure you were truly heard or respected, please listen to your instincts. Maybe you will want to talk it out with the clinician and give them a chance to rectify or clarify something, or maybe you will feel strongly enough to just move on. Either way, this is perfectly alright. You are the client, the consumer, and the one who will be doing all the hard work. You are choosing an expert companion, a guide, a coach—not a surgeon. If at any point in therapy you develop serious doubts, please pay attention to your instincts, speak up, and if need be, walk on. It's your life. You matter.

A wish:

Now that you are an informed "consumer," familiar with the workings of PTSD and equipped with some of the images and metaphors that others have found helpful, I hope that it will be possible for you to stay focused on your progress, or your loved one's progress, and unfazed when you encounter discouraging portrayals of PTSD in the media, cinema, or from advocacy groups. Some of these well-intentioned people have agendas or their own ways of looking at things. PTSD is not an inevitable consequence of a difficult experience, certainly not in a direct "cause and effect" fashion. It is not an "injury" like a broken bone that only a doctor can repair and that leaves you with a limp. While not everyone will be fortunate enough to recover fully and return to the same life as before, it is absolutely possible to move beyond trauma. It is not a permanent disability that one just "manages" their whole life long. It is a well understood, very human response to a difficult event or series of events that is treatable given some time, knowledge, and expert help. I hope I helped with the knowledge part.

As I write these final words, I am even more aware of the importance of a positive mindset as new scientific studies are being published every day. Self-fulfilling prophecies do exist, both in the positive and the negative directions. We now know that "mindset," another word for "expectations," plays a determining role in happiness, health, and success in most of life's endeavours. In essence, the message is: if you believe that you will overcome painful life experiences and grow from them, you will.

Resources

I would like to start by saying that the best reading materials are those recommended by your chosen therapist, as it is important that the approaches match. I also know the Internet is a jungle; without some guidance, it is hard to know which sources can be trusted. So here is my compromise: following are a few resources to get you started, whether you are battling PTSD yourself or you are supporting someone who is. You will note that they are all self-help resources; they are written for you, not the experts.

For more information on PTSD, on the therapies and medications available to treat it, and for more references for Dr. Foa's work, a good place to start is:

> Edna Foa, *et al.* (1999). Expert Consensus Guideline Series: Treatment of Posttraumatic Stress Disorder: *A Guide for Patients and Families. Journal of Clinical Psychiatry 60, Supplement 16*, pp. 69-76.

This article also contains a list of organizations and a self-administered questionnaire entitled "How can I tell if I have PTSD?" The article is available on the web at www.psychguides.com or as a handout from the Anxiety Disorders Association of America (ADAA).

Then, you can turn to an excellent workbook by Dr Foa and colleagues that walks you through every step of CBT treatment for PTSD. Its authors caution that it is best used in combination with treatment by a mental health professional:

> E. Foa, B. Rothbaum, and E. Hembree, 2007. *Reclaiming Your Life from a Traumatic Experience: a Prolonged Exposure Treatment Program Workbook.* Oxford University Press.

I also strongly recommend the works of Montreal's Dr. Pascale Brillon. They are highly readable, complete, and practical. She answers every question the readers may have with great compassion, whether they are the ones who faced trauma or those who love them. She is my inspiration. By the time you read this, I hope that her books will be available in English. If you read

French: *Se relever d'un traumatisme, Réapprendre à vivre et à faire confiance*, 2013. Éditions Québec-Livres; *Quand la mort est traumatique: Passer du choc à la Sérénité*, 2012. Éditions Québecor.

Another highly recommended read:

Tedeschi, R. G. & Moore, B. A. 2016. *The Post-Traumatic Growth Workbook*. Oakland, CA: New Harbinger.

Richard Tedeschi and Lawrence Calhoun coined the term Posttraumatic Growth (PTG) in the 1990s to describe the phenomenon where people experience positive transformation as they cope with trauma and life challenges. Their research shows that up to 70% of trauma survivors report some psychological growth. This growth occurs alongside PTSD; one does not wait for the other to improve. The new workbook will help the reader foster this growth.

More resources

The following resources are for everyone, not just people who are dealing with PTSD.

New resources to help you are coming out every day, including apps and videos. One YouTube video I love is called *Headstuck! What is Experiential Avoidance?* It explains beautifully why avoidance is limiting for everyone, and provides a good introduction to the ACT model.

There is now an atlas of emotions created by Paul Ekman which was created to be a "visual journey through the world of emotions". Good emotional management starts with recognizing and naming emotions. The atlas can be found at paulekman.com.

Please download a meditation app such as Buddhify2, Calm or Headspace, and make it a part of your day. There may be a small price, but being able to tap on your phone to access a short guided meditation to suit any activity or mood means that you can incorporate mindfulness practice into your daily life effortlessly.

If you are not convinced meditation is for you, ABC news correspondent and Dateline anchorman Dan Harris will tell you how he used meditation to overcome panic attacks and explain the science behind how it works in his book *10% Happier: How I Tamed the Voice in My Head, Reduced Stress Without Losing My Edge, and Found Self-Help that Actually*

Works – A True Story (2014, Harper Collins). His Big Think videos provide a great overview: meditation truly is for everyone.

You can also find some meditation exercises that are specifically designed to curb self-criticism and nurture self-compassion at self-compassion.org, Kristin Neff's website. Her research has shown that this very important skill can be learned.

If Kelly McGonigal's TEDTalk *How to Make Stress Your Friend* piqued your interest like it did mine, look for her book: *The Upside of Stress: Why Stress is Good for You and How to Get Good at It* (2015, Avery). It is described on the Amazon site as "a how-to guide for anyone who wants to tap into the biology of courage and the psychology of thriving under pressure.". It is about changing mindsets to become more resilient in life. It, too, is for everyone.